Searchlight
BOOKS

High-Tech Science

Explore

Bionics

Ainsley Nichols

Lerner Publications ◆ Minneapolis

Lerner Publications Company
An imprint of Lerner Publishing Group, Inc.
241 First Avenue North
Minneapolis, MN 55401 USA

For reading levels and more information, look up this title at www.lernerbooks.com.

Main body text set in Adrianna Regular.
Typeface provided by Chank.

Editor: Brianna Kaiser

Library of Congress Cataloging-in-Publication Data

Names: Nichols, Ainsley, author.
Title: Explore bionics / Ainsley Nichols.
Description: Minneapolis : Lerner Publications, [2024] | Series: Searchlight books. High-tech science | Includes bibliographical references and index. | Audience: Ages 8–11 | Audience: Grades 4–6 | Summary: "The science of bionics helps extend and save lives. Explore how people get inspired by animals and plants to improve human lives. Then learn about the technology used in modern bionics and its future"— Provided by publisher.
Identifiers: LCCN 2023006974 (print) | LCCN 2023006975 (ebook) | ISBN 9798765608913 (lib. bdg.) | ISBN 9798765616949 (epub)
Subjects: LCSH: Bionics—Juvenile literature. | Prosthesis—Juvenile literature. | Artificial organs—Juvenile literature. | BISAC: JUVENILE NONFICTION / Technology / Inventions
Classification: LCC TA164.2 .N53 2024 (print) | LCC TA164.2 (ebook) | DDC 003/.5—dc23/eng/20230320

LC record available at https://lccn.loc.gov/2023006974
LC ebook record available at https://lccn.loc.gov/2023006975

Manufactured in the United States of America
1-1009422-51569-3/31/2023

Table of Contents

Chapter 1

WHAT IS BIONICS?

Bionics is the science of building machines that mimic living things. Engineers try to solve problems by looking at how plants and animals solve the same problems. Then engineers build technology that does the same thing.

History of Bionics

Bionics is centuries old. Some of the earliest bionic devices were prostheses. They replaced body parts. Archaeologists found a wooden toe on an Egyptian mummy. The ancient toe was three thousand years old. It likely helped the person walk. A metal hand built in the 1500s allowed an injured German soldier to hold a sword again.

An ancient wooden toe prosthetic is on display in a museum in Egypt.

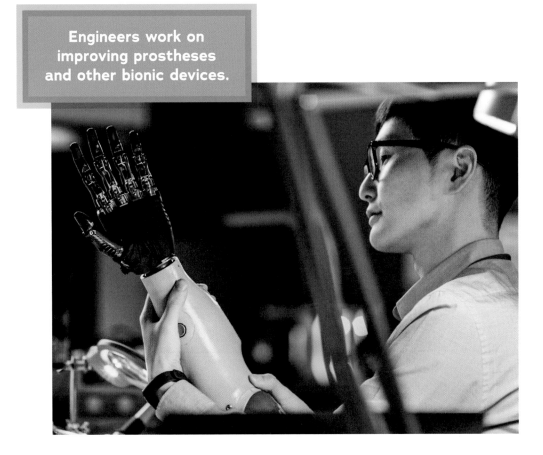

Early prostheses were difficult to use. They were heavy and could be hard to control. Over time, scientists have developed lighter prostheses. Advances in technology have made them easier to control.

Engineers have created other bionic devices used in fashion, travel, medicine, and many other parts of life. As researchers continue to study bionics, new technologies will make devices more affordable and more useful. The future of bionics is looking bright.

Chapter 2

INSPIRED BY NATURE

Bionics has been used to develop complex technology. But researchers can look to nature to come up with simple solutions to problems too.

Hook and Loop

In 1941, Swiss engineer George de Mestral was hunting when he noticed that his pants were covered in burrs.

Curious, he looked at the burrs under a microscope. They had tiny hooks that grasped onto the loops in the fabric of his pants.

De Mestral thought that he could make a fastener that copied the burrs' design. This hook-and-loop material would hold together but could be pulled apart with a little effort. He called his new material Velcro.

Burrs stick to boots and pants.

SANDALS WITH HOOK-AND-LOOP FASTENERS

The National Aeronautics and Space Administration (NASA) turned to the material to solve many of their problems. Astronauts used the hook-and-loop fasteners to hold their pockets closed and to secure scientific equipment in weightlessness. Back on Earth, people around the world use the fasteners on shoes, watches, and many other items.

Science Fact or Science Fiction?

Scientists have made a bionic kangaroo.

That's a fact! In 2014, a German company created a robot that mimics the jumping of real kangaroos. Kangaroos recover energy from one jump to fuel the next jump. They do this by using their tendons like springs. The bionic kangaroo uses a spring instead of a tendon. This technology may help save the energy that cars and other machines use.

Sonar

Researchers study echolocation in horseshoe bats to improve navigation systems for vehicles. The bats squeak as they fly. They listen as their squeaks bounce off objects. Their ears are so sensitive that they can tell the difference between a leaf and a moth.

A horseshoe bat uses echolocation to find food and avoid collisions.

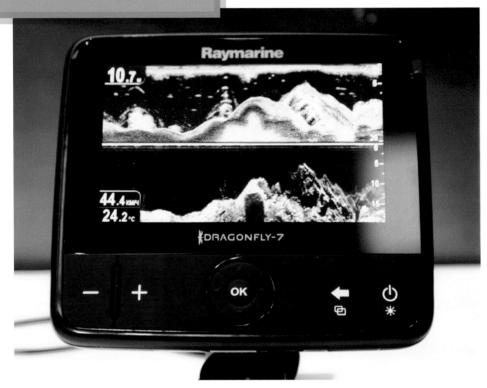

A sonar device for a boat

Ships, submarines, and other vehicles already use sonar, which acts like echolocation. But sonar equipment takes up a lot of space. Different machines are needed to measure different pieces of information. By watching horseshoe bats, engineers have developed more sensitive sonar technology that can measure multiple pieces of information. Because this sonar equipment takes up less space, it can fit into smaller vehicles, such as drones.

Chapter 3

BIONIC BODY

Bionic devices are common in medicine. A person may use a bionic device to make life easier. Some people have bionic devices that keep them alive.

Bionic Limbs

Some people are born without certain limbs, and some people lose limbs in accidents or because of disease.

They may choose to get a bionic prosthesis to replace the limb they lost. Bionic prostheses are myoelectric. They move by sensing signals from the person's muscles.

People who use traditional prostheses cannot feel their artificial limb. They need to watch what they are doing and may use too much or too little force when doing a task.

A man wearing a prosthetic arm holding a ball

PEOPLE DO DAILY TASKS WHILE WEARING PROSTHETIC ARMS.

In 2021, researchers built a new bionic arm. It sends signals to a person's muscles. The muscles relay these signals to the brain. Users can sense that their arm is moving or touching something. They can grab things without looking and correct mistakes quickly and easily.

Bionic Senses

Bionic devices can restore or provide other senses. Cochlear implants are one example. The cochlea is a coiled tube in the ear. It translates sounds into nerve signals. These signals then go to the brain. If the cochlea is damaged, a person can have hearing loss or no longer hear at all.

Part of a cochlear implant is outside of the ear, while another part is inside the ear.

COCHLEAR IMPLANT

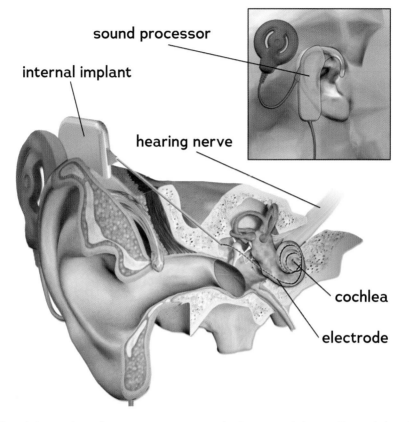

sound processor

internal implant

hearing nerve

cochlea

electrode

Cochlear implants go around the cochlea. Outside the ear are a microphone, sound processor, and transmitter. Surgeons place an internal implant and electrodes inside the ear.

The microphone collects sound from the outside world. The sound processor turns this sound into signals the brain can understand. The transmitter sends these signals through the skin. Then the internal implant collects them. Finally, the electrodes pass the signals through the hearing nerve. This nerve sends the signals to the brain. Hearing with a cochlear implant does not perfectly imitate hearing with a functioning cochlea. Although cochlear implants don't always work, they can sometimes help people hear better.

Bionic eye implants can help people with damaged retinas. The retina is in the back of the eye. A healthy retina turns images into electrical signals. The optic nerve sends these signals to the brain. When the retina is damaged, this process does not work and causes vision loss or blindness.

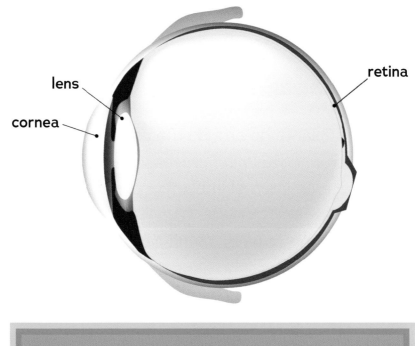

lens

cornea

retina

The cornea and lens bend light to focus an image. Once light reaches the retina, the retina turns the images into electrical signals.

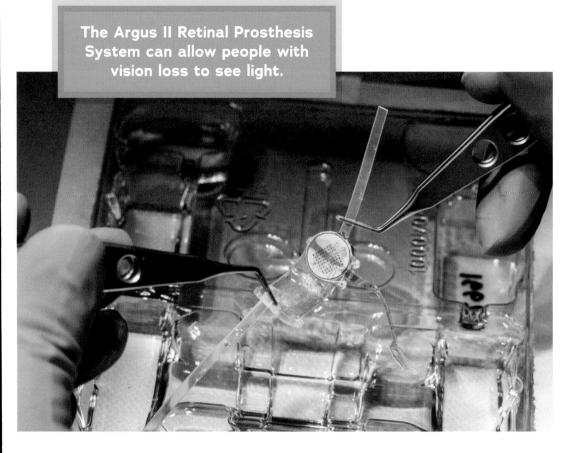

The Argus II Retinal Prosthesis System can allow people with vision loss to see light.

A bionic eye has a video camera attached to a pair of glasses. Users wear a video processing unit. It turns the camera's images into electrical signals. These signals go to an implant in the eye. The optic nerve passes these signals to the brain.

The bionic eye does not restore full vision. It can help people tell light from dark and avoid obstacles. They can tell if a person is in front of them. They can sense curbs and buildings.

Bionic Organs

Some people have organs that do not work properly. They might need an organ transplant. But the waiting list to receive some organs is very long. Artificial organs keep patients alive who might otherwise die waiting to receive a transplant.

Artificial hearts are mechanical pumps that replace the lower chambers of the heart. Valves control the blood flow. Some artificial hearts are powered by batteries inside the body. Others connect to an outside power source.

An artificial heart

STEM Spotlight

The need for transplants is far higher than the number of organs available. In 2022, over one hundred thousand people in the United States were waiting for an organ transplant. Scientists are looking to 3D printing to bridge the gap.

Objects can be created layer by layer with 3D printers. Some researchers think these printers can create organs that use living cells. This is called bioprinting. Bioprinting would help save many lives. But the technology will likely not be available for many years.

Kidneys filter waste from blood. When kidneys do not work properly, harmful wastes can build up. The usual treatment for kidney failure is dialysis. Patients must go to a clinic several times a week. Their blood flows through a large machine to filter it.

A bionic kidney can be implanted in the body. It uses human kidney cells to filter blood much like the organ would. It also balances the blood's salt, sugar, and water levels.

Scientist Shuvo Roy holds a model of a bionic kidney in 2013.

Chapter 4

CUTTING-EDGE BIONICS

Researchers are working to create new and improved bionic technologies. These efforts can open new possibilities in medicine and protect humans in dangerous situations.

Rescue Robots

Some researchers creating rescue robots studied the abilities of different animals. Scientists at the

University of California, Berkeley, saw how cockroaches can squeeze through small crevices by splaying their legs. These scientists built the CRAM robot, a palm-sized machine that can squeeze into tight spaces by mimicking the cockroach's movements. After an earthquake, CRAM robots could locate survivors in damaged buildings and identify safe entry points for human rescuers.

THE CRAM ROBOT (*TOP*) MIMICS THE WAY A COCKROACH (*BOTTOM*) MOVES.

WALK-MAN is a humanoid robot designed to support firefighters. WALK-MAN can be used in situations that are too dangerous for humans, such as when a building has a gas leak. The robot is remote-controlled. The operator receives information from sensors, cameras, and microphones on the WALK-MAN.

WALK-MAN in 2018

Bionic Neurons

Neurons send and receive signals
from the brain. Neurons form
networks throughout the body.
These networks keep the heart
beating and lungs breathing.
They allow people to move. When
neurons are damaged, health
problems can occur.

Scientists have made artificial neurons. They are small microchips. They can receive signals from neurons and pass them on to other neurons or organs. Scientists are working to implant artificial neurons in humans. The neurons may be able to prevent heart failure or improve memory. A person with paralysis may be able to walk again.

The microchips still need to be tested on humans and approved by the government. It will likely be years before people can begin using them. But they could make a huge impact on people's lives.

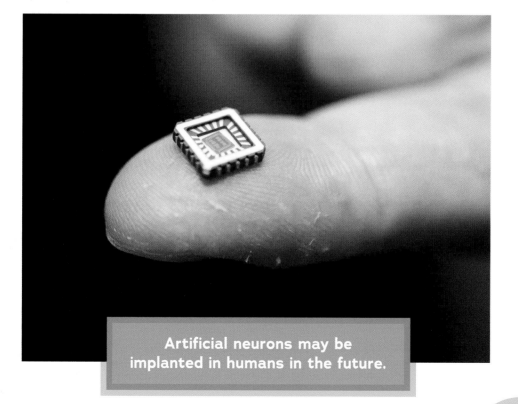

Artificial neurons may be implanted in humans in the future.

Science Fact or Science Fiction?

Scientists have built an artificial brain.

That's fiction! Scientists are not close to making an artificial brain. A human brain has about eighty-six billion neurons. Building a whole brain with artificial neurons would be too expensive and time-consuming. But technology continues to get faster, smaller, and cheaper. In the future, a bionic brain may be possible.

The Future Is Bionic

Bionics used to be the stuff of science fiction. But real-life bionics can be even more surprising than what you might find in a comic book or novel. Scientists are always looking for new ways to improve people's lives. There's no doubt that the field of bionics will continue to grow in the coming years.

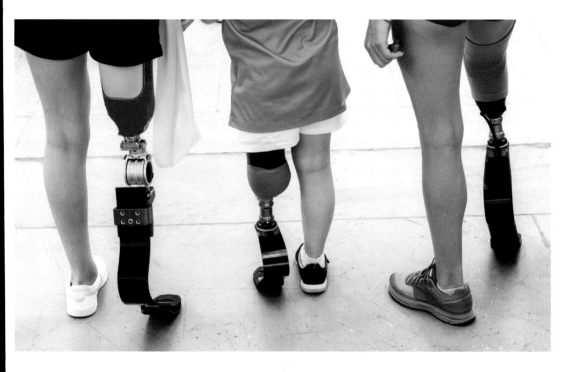

PROSTHESES CAN DIFFER BASED ON FUNCTION AND PRICE.

Glossary

bionics: the science of building machines that mimic living things

bioprinting: 3D printing that uses cells and other materials to create organs

cochlea: a hollow tube in the inner ear that converts sound vibrations into nerve impulses

mimic: to imitate closely

myoelectric: using electrical impulses in muscles to move a bionic part

optic nerve: a nerve that sends signals from the eye to the brain

prosthesis: an artificial body part

tendon: a cord of tissue that connects a muscle and a bone

transplant: to transfer an organ or tissue from one individual to another

Learn More

Biologically Inspired Robots
https://kidscodecs.com/bio-robots/

Britannica Kids: Bionics
https://kids.britannica.com/students/article/bionics/273221

Gutiérrez, Jolene. *Bionic Beasts: Saving Animal Lives with Artificial Flippers, Legs, and Beaks*. Minneapolis: Millbrook Press, 2021.

Health Headlines: New Bionic Arms Helping Children with Prosthetics
https://www.kplctv.com/2022/09/07/health-headlines-new-bionic -arms-helping-children-with-prosthetics/

Kaminski, Leah. *Bionic Bodies*. Fremont, CA: Full Tilt, 2021.

Walker, Tracy Sue. *Bionic Animals*. Minneapolis: Lerner Publications, 2024.

Index

Photo Acknowledgments

Image credits: Antonio Batinic/Shutterstock, p. 5; Gorodenkoff/Shutterstock, p. 6; Suzanne Tucker/Shutterstock, p. 8; GrashAlex/Shutterstock, p. 9; Carl Allen/Shutterstock, p. 11; ilmarinfoto/Shutterstock, p. 12; Yevhen Shkolenko/Alamy Stock Photo, p. 14; yurakrasil/Shutterstock, p. 15; Peakstock/Shutterstock, p. 16; Medical gallery of Blausen Medical 2014, courtesy of Wikimedia Commons (CC BY 3.0), p. 17; ttsz/Getty Images, p. 18; Phanie/Alamy Stock Photo, p. 19; Smile111222/Wikimedia Commons (CC BY-SA 4.0), p. 20; San Francisco Chronicle/Hearst Newspapers/Getty Images, p. 22; Tom Libby, Kaushik Jayaram and Pauline Jennings. Courtesy of PolyPEDAL Lab UC Berkeley., p. 24; Pier Marco Tacca/Getty Images, p. 25; Viaframe/Getty Images, p. 26; University of Bath, p. 27; Dmitry Markov152/Shutterstock, p. 29.

Cover: Witthaya Prasongsin/Getty Images.